CINCINNATI BENGALS

BY MARV ALINAS

The Child's World
childsworld.com

Published by The Child's World
800-599-READ • childsworld.com

Copyright © 2026 by The Child's World
All rights reserved. No part of this book may be reproduced or utilized in any form or by any means without written permission from the publisher.

Photography Credits
© Aaron Doster/AP Photo: 15; ChrisFloresFoto/Envato: football texture; Frame Craft 8/Shutterstock.com: 11; Jeff Dean/AP Photo: 19; Joe Robbins/AP Photo: 7, 17; julesrules/Shutterstock.com: 21; Michael Owens/AP Photo: cover, 2; oasisamuel/Shutterstock.com: 6, 9, (football); Scott Boehm/AP Photo: 12–13; Todd Rosenberg/AP Photo: 4–5

ISBN Information
9781503875173 (Reinforced Library Binding)
9781503875425 (Portable Document Format)
9781503876460 (Online Multi-user eBook)
9781503877504 (Electronic Publication)

LCCN
2024952239

ABOUT THE AUTHOR

Marv Alinas has written dozens of books for children. When she's not reading or writing, Marv enjoys spending time with her family and traveling to interesting places. Marv lives in Minnesota.

Cincinnati Bengals wide receiver Ja'Marr Chase

CONTENTS

The Team 4

The Colors 6

The Conference 8

The Stadium 10

The Football Field 12

Fun Fans 14

The Coaches 16

The Players 18

The Future 20

    Fast Facts 22
    Glossary 23
    Find Out More . . . 24
    Index 24

The Team

The Cincinnati Bengals are a football team. They play in Cincinnati, Ohio. They started in 1968.

The Cincinnati Bengals run onto the field to play football.

The Colors

Their team colors are orange, black, and white. Their **mascot** is a tiger. His name is Who Dey.

Bengals fans love to cheer, "Who dey, who dey, who dey think gonna beat dem Bengals? NOBODY!"

Who Dey attends lots of events off the football field.

The Conference

The Bengals are in the AFC North. The AFC stands for American Football **Conference**. There are three other teams in the AFC North.

The Baltimore Ravens, the Cleveland Browns, and the Pittsburgh Steelers are also in the AFC North.

The Stadium

The Bengals play at Paycor **Stadium**. It opened in 2000. It is nicknamed "the Jungle." It can hold more than 65,000 people.

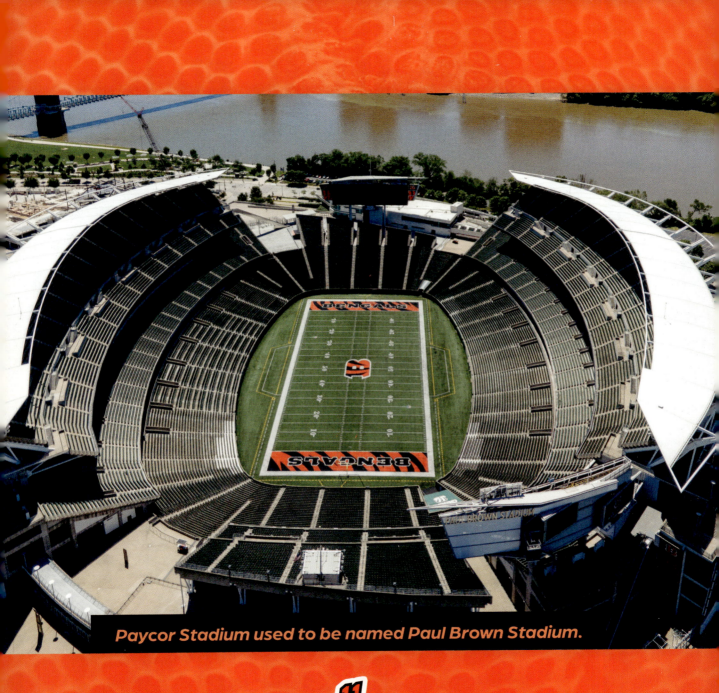

Paycor Stadium used to be named Paul Brown Stadium.

The Football Field

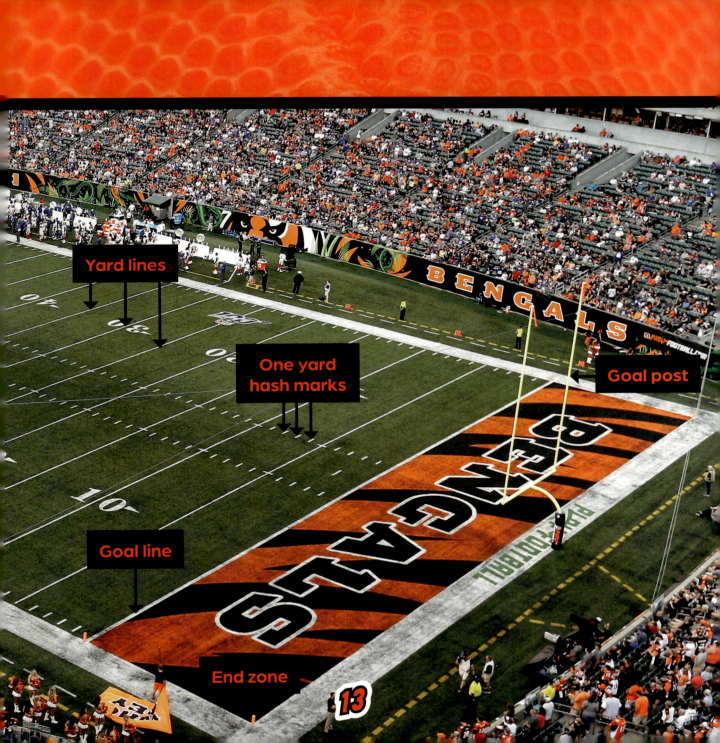

Fun Fans

Fans of the Bengals love to wear the team's colors. Some paint their faces like tigers. Many people wear a **jersey** with the number of their favorite player.

The Coaches

The Cincinnati Bengals have had ten head coaches since they began. Zac Taylor is the current coach. He has been the head coach since 2019.

Taylor worked with other NFL teams before becoming the Bengals' coach.

The Players

Many great players have been part of the Cincinnati Bengals. Some past greats include Chad "Ochocinco" Johnson, Anthony Muñoz, and Boomer Esiason.

Current Bengals stars are Ja'Marr Chase and Joe Burrow.

Ja'Marr Chase and Joe Burrow celebrate after a great play.

They are exciting to watch during games.

The Future

The Bengals have gone to the **Super Bowl** three times. They have never won. They will keep trying!

Super Bowl champions take home the Lombardi trophy.

FAST FACTS

- The Cincinnati Bengals play in Cincinnati, Ohio.

- The team is in the AFC North.

- Paycor Stadium can hold more than 65,000 people.

- The Cincinnati Bengals have never won a Super Bowl.

GLOSSARY

conference (KON-fur-enss): In sports, a conference is a grouping of teams.

jersey (JUR-zee): A jersey is a shirt sports players wear.

mascot (MAS-kot): In sports, a mascot is an animal, person, or thing that represents a team.

stadium (STAY-dee-um): A stadium is a large building where sports and concerts are held.

Super Bowl (SOO-pur BOWL): The Super Bowl is the championship game of the NFL.

FIND OUT MORE

In the Library

Anderson, Josh. *Cincinnati Bengals.*
Parker, CO: The Child's World, 2023.

Downs, Kieran. *The Cincinnati Bengals.*
Minneapolis, MN: Bellwether Media, 2024.

Whiting, Jim. *The Story of the Cincinnati Bengals.*
Mankato, MN: Creative Education, 2025.

On the Web

Visit our website for links about the Cincinnati Bengals:
childsworld.com/links

*Note to Parents, Caregivers, Teachers, and Librarians:
We routinely verify our web links to make sure they are safe
and active sites. So encourage your readers to check them out!*

INDEX

Burrow, Joe, 18

Chase, Ja'Marr, 2, 18
Cincinnati, 4
coach, 16
colors, 6
conference, 8

Esiason, Boomer, 18

fans, 6, 14
field, 12–13

Johnson, Chad
"Ochocinco," 18

Muñoz, Anthony, 18

players, 18

stadium, 10
Super Bowl, 20

Taylor, Zac, 16

Who Dey (cheer), 6
Who Dey (mascot), 6